# SCOTT JOPLIN
## BEST OF RAGTIME

Editor: Carol Cuellar

# CONTENTS

# SCHOOL OF RAGTIME

By SCOTT JOPLIN

**REMARKS** – What is scurrilously called ragtime is an invention that is here to stay. That is now conceded by all classes of musicians. That all publications masquerading under the name of ragtime are not the genuine article will be better known when these exercises are studied. That real ragtime of the higher class is rather difficult to play is a painful truth which most pianists have discovered. Syncopations are no indication of light or trashy music, and to shy bricks at "hateful ragtime" no longer passes for musical culture. To assist amateur players in giving the "Joplin Rags" that weird and intoxicating effect intended by the composer is the object of this work.

## Exercise No. 1.

It is evident that, by giving each note its proper time and by scrupulously observing the ties, you will get the effect. So many are careless in these respects that we will specify each feature. In this number, strike the first note and hold it through the time belonging to the second note. The upper staff is not syncopated, and is not to be played. The perpendicular dotted lines running from the syncopated note below to the two notes above will show exactly its duration. Play slowly until you catch the swing, and never play ragtime fast at any time.

## Exercise No. 2.

This style is rather more difficult, especially for those who are careless with the left hand, and are prone to vamp. The first note should be given the full length of three sixteenths, and no more. The second note is struck in its proper place and the third note is not struck but is joined with the second as though they were one note. This treatment is continued to the end of the exercise.

4

## Exercise No. 3.

This style is very effective when neatly played. If you have observed the object of the dotted lines they will lead you to a proper rendering of this number and you will find it interesting.

Slow march tempo (*Count Two*)

## Exercise No. 4.

The fourth and fifth notes here form one tone, and also in the middle of the second measure and so to the end. You will observe that it is a syncopation only when the tied notes are on the same degree of the staff. Slurs indicate a legato movement.

Slow march tempo (*Count Two*)

## Exercise No. 5.

The first ragtime effect here is the second note, right hand, but, instead of a tie, it is an eighth note: rather than two sixteenths with tie. In the last part of this measure, the tie is used because the tone is carried across the bar. This is a pretty style and not as difficult as it seems on first trial.

Slow march tempo (*Count Two*)

## Exercise No.6.

The instructions given, together with the dotted lines, will enable you to interpret this variety which has very pleasing effects. We wish to say here, that the "Joplin ragtime" is destroyed by careless or imperfect rendering, and very often good players lose the effect entirely, by playing too fast. They are harmonized with the supposition that each note will be played as it is written, as it takes this and also the proper time divisions to complete the sense intended.

**Slow march tempo** *(Count Two)*

# (The) Easy Winners

**By SCOTT JOPLIN**

*Introduction.*
*Not fast.*

"The Easy Winners" - 4 - 1

8

# (The) Crush Collision March

**Introd.**

BY SCOTT JOPLIN

**PIANO.**

**Tempo di Marcia.**

The Crush Collision March - 4 - 1

12

The noise of the trains while running at the rate of sixty miles per hour,

Whistling for the crossing,

Noise of the trains

Whistle before the collision

The collision

# (The) ENTERTAINER

**INTRO:**

*Not fast.*

By SCOTT JOPLIN

The Entertainer - 4 - 1

**Repeat 8va.**

The Entertainer - 4 - 4

# (The) CHRYSANTHEMUM

**Slow March Tempo.**

By SCOTT JOPLIN

The Chrysanthemum - 4 - 1

The Chrysanthemum - 4 - 2

The Chrysanthemum - 4 - 4

# ANTOINETTE

BY SCOTT JOPLIN

**Tempo di Marcia**

Antoinette - 4 - 1

**TRIO.**

# (The) CASCADES

BY SCOTT JOPLIN

*Tempo di Marcia.*

The Cascades - 4 - 1

The Cascades - 4 - 2

The Cascades - 4 - 4

# (The) STRENUOUS LIFE

By SCOTT JOPLIN

**Not fast.**

The Strenuous Life - 4 - 1

# SENSATION

BY SCOTT JOPLIN

**Tempo di marcia.**

Sensation - 3 - 1

**Trio.**

# (The) SYCAMORE

BY SCOTT JOPLIN

The Sycamore - 3 - 1

38

The Sycamore - 3 - 3

# (A) Breeze From Alabama

BY SCOTT JOPLIN

Not fast.

A Breeze From Alabama - 4 - 1

A Breeze From Alabama - 4 - 2

A Breeze From Alabama - 4 - 3

A Breeze From Alabama - 4 - 4

# ELITE SYNCOPATIONS

**Not fast.**

BY SCOTT JOPLIN

45

Elite Syncopations - 4 - 2

46

Elite Syncopations - 4 - 4

# "SOLACE"
## A MEXICAN SERENADE

BY SCOTT JOPLIN

"Solace" - 4 - 1

# PEACHERINE RAG

BY SCOTT JOPLIN

**Not too fast.**

Copyright © 1992 by BEAM ME UP MUSIC, c/o CPP/BELWIN, INC., Miami, FL 33014
International Copyright Secured     Made in U.S.A.     All Rights Reserved

54

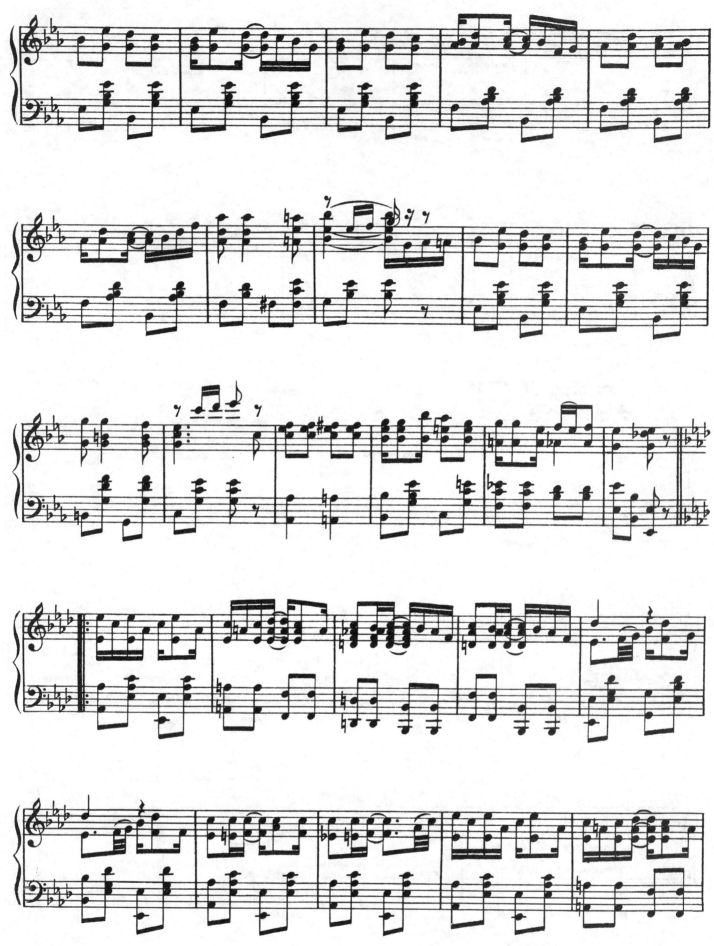

Peacherine Rag - 4 - 3

Peacherine Rag - 4 - 4

# ORIGINAL RAGS

**BY SCOTT JOPLIN**

Original Rags - 4 - 4

# Weeping Willow

**Not fast.**

BY SCOTT JOPLIN

Weeping Willow - 4 - 1

Weeping Willow - 4 - 4

# PALM LEAF RAG

BY SCOTT JOPLIN

Play a little slow

Palm Leaf Rag - 3 - 1

# CLEOPHA

BY SCOTT JOPLIN

Cleopha - 4 - 1

Cleopha - 4 - 4

# MARCH MAJESTIC

By SCOTT JOPLIN

**Tempo di marcia.**

March Majestic - 4 - 1

March Majestic - 4 - 4

# LEOLA

Notice! Don't play this piece fast. It is never right to play "rag-time" fast. Author

BY SCOTT JOPLIN

**Slow march tempo.**

Leola - 4 - 1

Leola - 4 - 2

# EUGENIA

Notice.!. *Dont play this piece fast,
It is never right to play "Ragtime" fast.*
Author.

By SCOTT JOPLIN

**Slow March Tempo** ♩ = 72

# BETHENA

By SCOTT JOPLIN

"Bethena" - 6 - 1

105

Binks' Waltz - 6 - 4

106

# HARMONY CLUB WALTZ

By SCOTT JOPLIN

INTRO.

109

Harmony Club Waltz - 4 - 2

Harmony Club Waltz - 4 - 4

# Please Say You Will

By SCOTT JOPLIN

1. Closed in the par-lor we are a lone _____
2. Oh Ma-mie loved one don't treat me so _____
3. Now we must part love I'll ask a-gain _____

Hap - py to be with one that I love _____
You have for-sak - en where will I go, _____
Don't let this plead - ing be all in vain _____

Please Say You Will - 4 - 1

I'll ask you kind — ly oh Ma - mie dove _____ Do
Bowed on my knees I pray once a - gain _____ For-
You know I love you why not for - give _____ For

speak just a few words to bind us in love _____
give me my loved one for I am to blame _____
my heart is brok - en oh please say you will _____

I will con - fess that I have been false _____
Once you were kind and kissed me so sweet _____
Let us a - gree love o - pen your heart _____

**Please Say You Will - 4 - 2**

113

114

*Chorus:*

Must I plead must I kneel and you not for-give_____

Has your heart love been sealed do you love me still_____

You have al - -ways been true now why not for-give_____ I

don't love none but you please say you will_____

# (A) Picture Of Her Face

By SCOTT JOPLIN

This life is ver - - y sad to me, a sor - row fills my
I'll ne'er for - get the days I've pass'd, with Grace, so kind and

heart,_____ My sto - ry I will tell to you, from me my
true,_____ She was to me each day more joy than all the

A Picture Of Her Face - 4 - 1

love did part,_____ The vil - lage church bell sad - ly tolled, the
girls I knew,_____ My love for her will ne'er grow cold though

one I loved had died,_____ She was a treas - ure more than
she has passed a - way,_____ I'll love her still when I am

gold, when she was by my side._____ But now she's gone be -
old e'en to my dy - ing day._____ But now I must con -

- yond re - call, in a si - lent tomb she sleeps, _____ The
- tent my - self, her mem - o - ry to love,_____ For

**A Picture Of Her Face - 4 - 2**

118

one  I  loved  yet  best  of  all  has  left  me  here  to  weep;_____ Though
Grace  the  dar - ling  of  my  heart  is  in  the  land  a - bove;_____ But

death  so  ruth - less  stole  my  love,  my  dear  and  on - ly  Grace,_____ I've
still  to  cheer  me  at  my  home  an  im - age  of  dear  Grace,_____ Is

yet  a  treas - ure  in  this  world,  A  pic-ture  of  her  face._____ It
all  the  treas - ure  I  now  have,  A  pic-ture  of  her  face._____

*Refrain:*

brings  joy  to  me_____  when  oft - times  sad  at  heart,_____ Her

*A Picture Of Her Face - 4 - 3*

pic-ture I can see, _____ And sad thoughts then de - part; _____ Al -

- though my love is dead, _____ My on - ly dar - ling Grace, _____ My

eyes are oft - times looking on A picture of her face. _____

# RAG-TIME DANCE

By SCOTT JOPLIN

**Not too fast**

Rag-Time Dance - 4 - 1

Rag-Time Dance - 4 - 2

**NOTICE :** To get the desired effect of "Stop Time," the pianist will please <u>Stamp</u> the heel of one foot heavily upon the floor at the word "Stamp". Do not raise the toe from the floor while stamping.

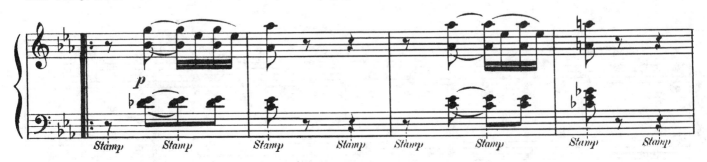

Stamp   Stamp   Stamp   Stamp   Stamp   Stamp   Stamp   Stamp

Rag-Time Dance - 4 - 4

# Sarah Dear

Words by HENRY JACKSON

BY SCOTT JOPLIN

**Sarah Dear - 4 - 1**

And as I a - wake from my slum - ber deep,___ I'm still
And you cause a thought to come to my mind,___

think-ing of Sa - rah dear;_____ When
you my Sa - rah dear;_____

e'er I get a glimpse___ of you dear girl,___ my
I've a ques -tion that I would ask of you,___ you can

126

heart is filled__ with glee;_____ When you are with me__ it's
make me hap-py through life;_____ And when we're a-lone__ the

pleas-ure you see,__ with you I long to be.__
truth will be known,__ I'll ask you to be my wife.__

*Chorus:*

O! you are my Sa - rah dear,__ the sun-light of__ my

soul;__ You have won my heart__ and hand__

Sarah Dear - 4 - 3

# SOMETHING DOING

SCOTT JOPLIN
SCOTT HAYDEN

Intro.
Not fast.

Something Doing - 4 - 1

Something Doing - 4 - 4

# SWIPESY

By SCOTT JOPLIN
and
ARTHUR MARSHALL

Swipesy - 4 - 2

134

Swipesy - 4 - 4

136

# Sun Flower Slow Drag

**INTRO.**
*Not fast.*

# Heliotrope Bouquet

*N.B. Do not play this piece fast. It is never right to play "Ragtime" fast. Composers.*

By SCOTT JOPLIN
and LOUIS CHAUVIN

**Slow March Tempo.**

Piano.

Heliotrope Bouquet - 4 - 1

157

Heliotrope Bouquet - 4 - 3

Heliotrope Bouquet - 4 - 4

# FELICITY RAG

SCOTT JOPLIN
and
SCOTT HAYDEN.

Tempo di Marcia.

# REFLECTION RAG

By SCOTT JOPLIN

Slow March Tempo.

Reflection Rag - 2 - 1

# (The) FAVORITE

By SCOTT JOPLIN

*Slow March Tempo.*
**INTRO.**

The Favorite - 3 - 1

168